Life Could Be Verse

By
Tony Hibberd

Published and distributed by

Nounagain Publishing
P.O. Box 10014
Halstead C09 2WS

Phone **07733282143**

www.nounagain.com

Email: Verselife@Nounagain.com

For details of how to order further copies of this book please see page 139

ISBN No.
978-0-9557846-0-6

First Edition 2008

All material in this book is protected by copyright and may not be reproduced or electronically stored without the written consent of the author Tony Hibberd

© 2008 Tony Hibberd

Life Could Be Verse

A dedication

*To all the friends and family who believed
In me as a writer and who's constant pestering
For me to get these works published.*

I say a big thank you

*If however they have not been published
And nobody is reading this dedication
I would then like to say to the above*

Told you so…

Thanks

Tony Hibberd

Contents

Worthless Wordsmith	8
Vintage Model	10
Bavarian Beauty	13
Easy Travel	15
Peace and Quiet	17
Metric Mayhem	18
London Winter Wonderland	21
The Hit	23
Carroll's Dream	26
The Sage	27
Literary Lightweight	29
The Phantom of the Opera	30
The Garden Party	32
Me Myself I	37
A Stranger Comes Calling	39
Indecision	41
Menopause	43
Man of Power	45
DIY	47
Remember Me	49
The Death of Football	51
Macbeth	53

The Myth of Recycling	55
Failure	57
Tiger	58
Mind Control	59
Two Friends	61
A Hole Lot of Trouble	64
Life Could Be Verse	69
The Great Fire	70
Way to Go	73
All Quiet	74
Hidden Love	76
Time	77
A penitent Man	78
Foreigner	80
Digitally Damaged	82
Night Must Come	84
Digitally Damaged Too	88
The Day After	89
A Happy Thought to Start the Day	90
Sun Arise No More	92
Hail Caesar	94
Tell Me Lies	96

Hamlet Revisited	99
Inevitable	102
A Family Tree	103
Spare a Thought	108
Conflict	111
Nursery Rhyme	114
Desert Island Risks	115
Dogs of War	117
The Meeting	119
Dead End	121
Solitude	124
Trust Me	125
Wyrd or What	127
The Highwayman	129
Dream On	132
End Credits	134
Bonus Poem	135
Ordering Information	139

Worthless Wordsmith

You know, some of my best friends are words
Either single or gathered in herds
Numbers are fine,
Algebraic or sine
Seed numbers and prime are just for the birds
Or brain food for mathematical nerds

A memorable quote or some old rustic phrase,
Puts a smile on my face, I'll be happy for days
Every page that I turn,
The more words do I learn
I gain self-esteem with worship and praise
As I pass through my biographical phase

A per chant for posh words of the linguistical kind
Can alter perceptions in anyone's mind
They may think you dim
Or decidedly grim
But speak eloquent rubbish and you'll surely find
No matter how hostile, their perceptions will blind

It may be I'm lonely, but I'm never alone
Whilst my brain imitates a great prosaic tome
My friends have all gone,
They never stay long
Some down the pub, the others off home
I could always text them, wow, words on the phone

Thesaurus and dictionary are my greatest mates
Forever a comfort through monotonous debates
Prose is for fun and never a chore,
With my verbal dexterity, I'm thrilled to the core
I unleash verbose tirades of my pleasures and hates
My ambitions are high now, I will challenge the fates

Things are not good, my words will not fuse
I sacrificed all for the sake of my muse
My means are so short; I'm now living in squalor
This cannot be right, me, a wordsmith, a scholar
My writing is shoddy it earns naught but scorn
I, William Shakespeare, wish I'd never been born.

Vintage Model

The car parked outside has seen better days
Its presence affects me in many ways
The windows now opaque with grime
They shone like glass in a former time

Rusticles feast beneath the paint
Once vibrant colours now dull and feint
The furry dice threadbare and bald
Ancient icons of dreams so bold

Arches flaring above alloy wheels
Manual radio emits short wave squeals
Eight track, bulky, forever hissing
Wind down windows, one handle missing

Leather seats of black seduction
Now emulate a hag's complexion
A straight exhaust for feral growl
Struggles now with meek meow

Short change gear stick with Saint Christopher knob
Fresh air turtle, now just a blob
Shagged piled carpets on the floor
Frayed string handles, on left hand door

Not always has it been this way
This erstwhile chariot once had its day
So proud and sleek, this Austin Maxi
A family car, the children's taxi

Whilst interior's filled with joy and glee
Drove car free travelers' to infinity
A sign of hope, a thing of joy
It played its part in girl meets boy

I stare quite wistful once again
The rain rivuleting towards the drain
Our lives are similar yours and mine
We're fast deteriorating and short of time

As we huddle in the wet and cold
My thoughts return to those days of old
We were a team, the classic pair
The highway kings I do declare

British engineering at its best
You never failed the Government test
No made in China in those days
Great British strikes for better pay

Petrol at an affordable price
No traffic calming, that was nice
To motor then was sheer delight
No camera flashes in the night

Back to reality, the dream must end
My thoughts approach the final bend
Off to the scrap yard you must soon go
The irony not lost; I'll soon be in tow

Bavarian Beauty

The morning mists roll down the hill
Form ethereal lakes as hollows fill
Flora drenched, its job now done
Starts evaporating in the sun

Shadows now replace the mist
As mound and light fulfill their tryst
Tree shaped shadows avoid the sun
And mark the hours, one by one

No dark satanic mills do stand
In Bavaria's green and pleasant land
No dog eat dog, no rats to race
Just work the land at nature's pace

Though conscious of the world outside
No locals to its ways are tithed
The silence slowly fills the dells
Disturbed only by the cattle bells

The scene outside, Beethoven's delight
Pastoral peace in midday light
The sun moves on across the sky
Past pastures where the löwenzahn lie

The distant mountains form a bed
For proud Apollo to rest his head
Now evening falls with velvet shroud
And sleepy hills are crowned with cloud

The cattle silent, the pastures still
As night comes rolling down the hill
Folk will sleep without a care
No evil stalks this land so fair

Easy Travel

One hours queuing to easy check in
Two more hours before boarding begins
Somehow this process doesn't seem right
A three hour delay for a one hour flight

We've tax free shopped and eaten our fill
With pockets empty, we shun brimming tills
Beer fuelled youths both vulgar and brash
Looks like we're flying with Euro trash

Boarding call is overdue
Allows final visit to the loo
Business type talks loud, hands free
Terms re-negotiated in mid pee

Fight for seats as we board the plane
Not quite steerage but feels the same
Aircraft refueled amid signs and warnings
We contribute to global warming

The craft backs out from its docking space
Led by a guide at walking pace
How come pilots that the world traverse
Can fly a plane, but not reverse?

We gather speed, the engines roar
A stewardess points to too few doors
But if we should crash in watery plight
We have a whistle and a light

A steep ascent now above the cloud
Which close resembles snow fresh ploughed
From the corner of my eye
I glimpse a Care Bear passing by

That wing it moves, just watch it shake!
What will we do if it should break?
I'm not quite sure if we would dive
Or wait up here till help arrives

We settle now our palms still damp
And settle back to enjoy the cramp
Drinks are proffered and snacks so lite
For a similar sum paid for the flight

The downward descent the final approach
On foreign lands we now encroach
Our journey over, money well spent
These no frills airlines are heaven sent.

Peace and Quiet

All is quiet no birds do sing
I lie here, quite still, pondering
I hear no children passing by
So here I lay and wonder why?

No voice disturbs me from my thought
Achievements all have come to naught
As I think, my eyes are closed
I lie here now in calm repose

My thoughts now turn to life's sweet merits
As preached to us by church and clerics
The medics too have got it wrong
As they'll find out before too long

The tender touch no more is mine
Thoughts of friends help pass the time
Life's greatest mystery revealed to me
No bad achievement aged fifty three

So here I lie now never seen
Six foot below the funeral green
If I could move I would surely scream
Death is real, it's not a dream

Metric Mayhem (synopsis)

Whilst designing and ordering materials for a DIY project, I found myself measuring in both Imperial and Metric.

The confusion was further enhanced when I quoted to a worthy purveyor of builder's materials
That I required seven 3 meter lengths of 100mm by 50mm timber and 2 kilos of 150mm nails.

This had not been that easy to convert for me but I always aim to please.

After a short pause and a scratch of his noggin the jolly, burly wood smith replied.

"Ok so yer want seven lengths of four be two and 4 pound of six inch nails,

yeah."

Metric Mayhem

I hate Metric, its Metric I hate
I do the conversions and get in a state
What's wrong with Inches, a Foot and a Chain?
Kilometers Meters, sod that for a game

Mention give em an Inch and they'll take a Mile
People know what you mean, it causes a smile
Say offer a Metre and they take a K
You're given blank looks and they just walk away

When I walk half a Mile to the pub Friday night
My beers half a Litre, it doesn't sound right
The stall outside though is something to treasure
I can still buy my seafood in old Quart sized measures

When talking of vertically challenged friends
Short arse or Half-pint is the name that appends
It looses the edge the humour does teeter
If you refer to that person as one point five Metre

The kids, they seem happy with bases of ten
Litres and Tonnes will not flummox them
So each to their preference whatever way fits
I know where my camp lies; I'm with the old gits

London Winter Wonderland

The day is o'er for office folk
Leaving work amidst text and talk
The denizens of London's City
Bereft of corporate identity
Homeward bound, commuting throng
Back to suburbs, where they belong

Tonight is different, something's strange
The gods have acted, it's all arranged
A thundering flash, a brilliant light
A Thor like herald that starts the fight
Pace now quickens as human tide
Seek refuge or shelter in which to hide.

The wind now rises to a gale
The surrounding air fast turning pale
Snowflakes, huge, go swirling by
A stinging beauty beheld by eyes
As faces lift to leaden cloud
The city's wrapped in still white shroud

Gridlocked streets now solid packed
Canned commuters, Congestion taxed
Radio blurbs foretelling doom
Night riders acquiesce with gloom
No match girl found on any street
Replaced now with "Big Issue!" greet

As time goes by the City sleeps
The snowy flurries turn to sleet
Travelers traveled and most are well
All have tales of travel hell
Some pass their nights on frozen rails
Others peruse their car's entrails

Just once a year this fate unfolds
Heedless of the woe foretold
Our city worker never bowed
Nor with any common sense endowed
For on the morrow, through the rain
They'll endure the torture once again.

The Hit

Imagine you're a bird on high
What scene attracts your clear sharp eye?
Contemporary sprawling dirty town
Encircling autumnal park so brown
Figures perform an urban dance
As something catches in your glance.

A tall brick tower that looms so high
A place where humans live and die
Upon the roof so flat and square
A figure, prone, just lying there
Clothed in garb as black as night
Long metal object glints sunlight

Now change perspective, leave feathered host
Enter black figure like possessive ghost
You see what he sees through his eyes
You think what he thinks, there's no surprise
Feel now his anticipation
Tempered by slight trepidation

Still as still you hold the stance
As if immersed in karmic trance
Your right eye pressed upon the sight
The stock and trigger held nice and tight
Cold steel barrel is filled with death
The morning chill steams bated breath

Your victim soon, you know will come
To die there in the morning sun
One shot is all the time you need
For him there is eternity
Something stirs now, the time is here
Suppress the ever-rising fear

Pressure mounts upon the trigger
Beads of sweat now growing bigger
The victim now within crosshairs
A small sharp crack splits morning air
A round dark hole stains victims head
Embrace the floor, already dead

The deed now done, its time to go
No remorse, no hint of woe
Just a way of having fun
No thought of victim's mate or son
The squirrel's body starts to cool
As the boy re-sights now, on the school

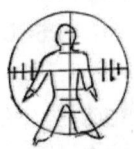

Carroll's Dream

A dream, it comes to me mid sleep
As if some tryst I've failed to keep
Something lost I cannot find
In dark recesses of my mind

I search in vain, there's nothing here!
Panic rises through my fear
Perhaps I'm lost or maybe late
Insecure in somnambulist state

My eyes, they dance to REM
A dreamer's form of requiem
My limbs now twitch, I thresh about
Till I awake with resounding shout

The dream, it fades, the dark decays
My mind retreads familiar pathways
But what was that on the edge of sight
A watch bearing rabbit of purest white?

The Sage

My name is Hakkan, I'm an eight year old boy
I live with my family on the banks of great Hoy
Too young yet to join in the great tribal hunts
Or even go fishing on our fleet of small punts

My duty decreed until I come of age
Is to listen and learn from our tribal sage
Great grandfather to me so I've been told
All I know is, he seems incredibly old

Daily we sit on the banks of great Hoy
He tells me the lore of when he was a boy
His life seemed so different, so removed from our own
But from his recounting, future wisdom is drawn

At night in our cave, his words fill my head
As I try to make sense of the things he has said
No animals harnessed to pull around corn
But by mystical force the carts were all drawn

I understand not, some of the things that he says
Like when he explains turning night into days
Creation of fire, I was taught while quite young
He speaks of warmth by taming the sun

When we lay by the lakeside, my sage is asleep
My mind it does wander as I try to seek
The truth of his memories from so long in the past
Distortion of truth?, has time made a mask?

The rain is still acid, he claims to know why
Strange looks on his face as the birds pass us by
Weird words does he use like forest and leaves
And sorcery he calls electricity

My wish it is simple, I wish I could contrive
A conveyance through time, so I could arrive
In the era he talks of with passion and awe
Before the nuclear attacks of 2004

Literary Lightweight

Keats is just cobblers, Chaucer is crap
Just give me a book by Andy Mc Nab
He knows his own purpose, he knows where he stands
He strides through this world and kills with his bare hands

Aristotle is senile and Homer is pap
These pretentious buggers deserve a good slap
My kind of author is the great Ed Mc Bain
To whom not even Dante can offer a flame

De foe is a deadbeat but no worse than duca't
A boy befriends convict, what the Dickens was that?
Give me a story to get my teeth into now
Bram Stoker has failed me, Jane Austin's a sow

Shelley is alright, the bird, not the fool
When the crowds fight the monster, I found that quite cool
Tell me now mother and fill me with glee
When will we next visit the pre school library?

Phantom of the Opera

A year ago whilst in some small town
I sought entertainment to clear the frown
The town's centre, it housed hostelries
Along with a theatrical repository

I took a dram, then by and by
Ambled next door, tickets to buy
The theatre, shabby, had seen better days
But I was a sucker for more offbeat plays

The tale, it was good the cast gave their all
By the time the play finished I was fully enthralled
The story enacted was one of some dread
Recounting a mansion staffed by the dead

The play finally ended with a twist in the end
The servants, the ghosts, drove their boss round the bend
So back to my room with some little sorrow
As my business was finished, I return home tomorrow

A year has since passed and I'm back in that place
I'm staying the night so my steps I retrace
The pub, it is found still in the same place
But as of the theatre, there is not a trace

The street plainly empty, no pedestrian about
So I hail a black cab with a wave and a shout
The driver pulls over and stops with a jerk
Drops down the window and gives me a smirk

"I'm looking for a theatre; I'm sure close at hand"
"You are correct sir, you must mean the Grande
But that was burnt down, ten years or more
Nothing like that, around here anymore"

"Burnt down" said I, "this cannot be"
He said "it was a tragedy"
"Eight people burnt to death that night
All actors who tried the fire to fight

A cabbie blamed, then duly hung
Found out later, they hanged the wrong one"
I glanced behind me to again see the site
As I turned back a cold wind smite

Before me was a clear empty street
No cab, no people, just falling sleet
Trudging back with fear's cold enthrall
Had I just witnessed the last curtain call

The Garden Party

Invites sent, there's no recourse
Forgotten friends will hear remorse
Scour the list just one more time
Exactly where to draw the line

Frightened mustard, cowering cress
Beaten eggs endure duress
Salads tossed with no compassion
Nouvelle cuisine in petit fashion

Ranks of glass stand all in line
Await fulfillment from Bacchus vine
The meat and fish are pungent still
Fresh loaves have memories of the mill

Grass manicured and closely shorn
Blades, by blades are cruelly torn
Hedges hedged and trees cut back
Nature abjures the sustained attack

Seating sited and tables too
Misdemeanors removed from loo
Fuel stacked up and kinder wood
Bonfire, echoes, ancient manhood

Ceramic disks give the table grace
Every guest will know their place
Silver glitters in the sun
Elegance donned for everyone

The scene is set the stage is ready
We now await the player's entry
Come one, come all the tables set
Join the dance of etiquette.

Car doors slam as a final pact
Grateful occupants arrive in tact
Greetings shouted as they reach the gate
A cacophony of the party state

Doorbell rings and knocker bounced
As every guest is thus announced
Aunties, uncles, kith and kin
Kids and pets enhance the din

Kisses, hugs, handshakes galore
As required by social law
The throng now having eased their cramp
Now in the kitchen do encamp

With glass in hand and arm in arm
The host herds them up and keeps them calm
To manicured garden they then are led
They've all been watered, now to be fed.

A bar-b-que with embers glowing
Heats succulent meat with juices flowing
Fish gently cooked, tastes like a dream
Molten butter now the piscine stream

The sun rides on across the sky
And slowly red hot charcoal dies
The guest now finished with their platters
Talk in groups, of trivial matters

The clouds act cirrus flecked with red
As swallows dance above our heads
The evening comes as well it might
Its time the chimenea to light

Some guest leave, with regretful tones
Their young offspring are reduced to moans
Others stay to enjoy the night
They gather round the fiery light

The brandies poured, the tales are told
So enraptured, no-one feels the cold
Friends as one, no need for others
We bond now deeper than with our own mothers

And so darkness wraps its velvet shroud
The flora and fauna heads all bowed
The last log burns, its time to leave
With final hugs, it's hard to breathe

The guests all gone, the hosts alone
Standing on the lawn new mown
They walk slowly back up the path
Tomorrow they'll clear the aftermath

"Its hard work", says one, quite quiet
"I hope they all enjoyed the night"
The other says, with mirthful grin
"We'll soon find out when we do it agin"

And so our heroes leave the stage
The book of life has another page
All lives have woe and fretful ghosts
But are put aside by jovial hosts

Any person who throws a party
Be them rich, poor or just plain arty
Are rightly seen as leading lights
Because we, as guests enjoy these nights

Me Myself I

Look you close upon my mask
I'll tell you now what you may see
A man with strength, wit and guile
Protector of the family

Look you close upon my mask
See now how the world sees me
A hunter in contemporary forests
A person of ability

Look you close upon my mask
A child's view now, as you can see
A jolly clown who never frowns
A figure of hilarity

Look you close upon my mask
And see now what my peers perceive
Slow to anger quick to laugh
A calm collected entity

Look you close upon my mask
Mirror's image reflecting back at me
Forgotten roots an unknown face
Completely alien identity

Look now deep into my eyes
See the child that therein lies
Smothered by so many covers
No one ever hears the cries

Look now deep into my eyes
See the wrath, volcanic fires
White hot, deep, but kept in check
Eruptions one day will arise

Look now deep into my eyes
Unsure of where the true path lies
The traveller within, halters never sure
But waits till luck or fate decides

Look now deep into my eyes
I'll tell you now what you will see
My soul protected by your love
The keeper of my sanity

Look you now at the person whole
See both parts are fast entwined
The answers right in front of you
This fact is true for all mankind

A Stranger Comes Calling

The night of nights is drawing near
The eve of Saints and unknown fears
Will o the Wisps stalk the Fen
Under baleful stares from wicker men
Hags on high, on brooms, backs bent
Are gathering now with foul intent

Dead mans fingers push through the earth
Deadly nightshade pollutes the turf
Dread figures glimpsed in winding shrouds
As waxing moon cowers behind the clouds
All must come they know not why
An annual web that traps the fly

Creatures of light have no domain
Only denizens born of brimstone and flame
The bells will peal with darkened hue
Just pray they do not toll for you
Cats, black as night avoid your way
Bats celebrate the death of day

The call to you is loud and clear
Come meet us on this night of fear
Join us in our fearful quest
Till late you'll find there is no rest
Experience sights o so macabre
Be sure to don appropriate garb

Fear is rising, sweat so cold
Prepare as destiny now unfolds
At unknown portal we knock and wait
Kind or cruel, it's down to fate
Door slowly opens with eerie creak
We shout as one now, **Trick or Treat**

Indecision
(For Stacy)

I used to be indecisive
But now I'm not so sure
It used to take me half an hour to exit my front door
Should I put the cat out?
Or simply let it burn
Should I take the rubbish hence, or is today his turn

I make it through the front door
This fills me with some glee
But is it safe to go to work or do I need a pee
I've made it to the front gate
I'm making such good time
The problem I now have to face, is to use his car or mine

Decision is so difficult
I'll toss a coin to choose
Heads is best, no tails this time, but what if I should lose
I think I'll walk, a pleasant day
The sun will please my face
I hope to reach my workplace before I my steps retrace

I must have forgotten something
But just what, I am unsure
Life is hell, it's just not nice, the thoughts that I endure
I reach a junction in the road
Oh no! Where should I cross?
Its no use using coins again, I lost the bloody toss

I'm almost there, not far to go
I see the BBC
I falter at the final fence, shall I show them my ID
What if this, or what if that,
Which is the better way?
I'd better get my act together or no racing tips today

Menopause

I'm close to reaching fifty-five
I'm told a changing time
Trapped inside a body
That seems no longer mine
My anger always simmering
With short tempered fiery blast
I'm sure I was more placid
In the not so distant past

No nightly heating needed
Cos I'm sweating like a pig
And when I now appraise myself
My ankles seem so big
When I least expect it,
Succumb to white hot flush
Feel just like a schoolchild
In the midst of loves first blush

What is really going on?
I dearly need to know
I really should be grateful
No sign of monthly flow
If confronted with wilting flower
Or pictures of Brad Pitt
I cry the tears in torrents
I completely go to bits

My hormones seem rebellious
As if on holiday
I scan the women's magazines
To see what agony aunts say
My friends have no sympathy
They laugh at me, and joke
But I just can't help myself
I'm such a sensitive bloke!

Man of Power

The wizard strode across the years
Oblivious to the strife and tears
As common in the magic clan
Ignores the plight of mortal man

In darkened tomes his interests lie
Symbolic icons catch his eye
No time to heal the people's ill
Scant sympathy does he ere feel

In castle high, in tallest tower
On golden throne he sits and glowers
From Mother's grief to Warlord's hate
No interest in the human state

The wizard's king of his domain
There forever to remain
His people starve and have no hope
Punishment served by the rope

Ancient rituals thus performed
By dark gowned servants, well informed
People sent to distant wars
Soldiers dying for ancient scores

Many acolytes serve him with glee
All bowing low to his mastery
They praise and caper at his side
They little care for folk outside

The wizard and his servile ranks
Will now and then give God their thanks
For power that grows with increment
In his stronghold we call Parliament

DIY

Whilst concluding home decorating
A job I find invigorating
Rewiring lights, beginning to tire
I found that I had a spare wire.

So I gave an exploratory pull
To see if it would come out in full
To my surprise it moved with ease
And soon had cable up to my knees

A momentary jerk and a bursting of plaster
The fuse box appeared, what a disaster
But I'm not at all phased, I continue to tug
When the electricity meter lands on the rug

Not even slowing when out of the hole,
Comes a big grey transformer attached to its pole
With a boom and a roar like the end of creation
I've manage to pull the local sub station

The cable now larger, insulators of nylon
I struggle indeed with the massive steel pylon
This must be the end, there's surely no more
But my words are soon drowned out by the turbine's loud roar

This is enough, I need a Contractor
As I come face to face with a nuclear reactor
Yellow pages I scan, electrical service espy
Could this possibly be my last DIY

Remember Me

As I rapidly approach my end
I find that time is not my friend
So much to do, so little time
No fame or fortune will be mine

Too late the hero for to be
Life had mundane plans for me
If I had lived in days of yore
I'd slaughtered dragons by the score

Maybe a General in wars gone by
Not leaving any men to die
A one armed Admiral, perhaps one eye
Kismet Hardy, before I die

A space man, trek the final frontier
A lunar lemming, I hear you jeer
I prefer to think a cosmic poet
"Its life Jim, but not as we know it"

A lumberjack so tall and straight
Who strips the forests at alarming rate
A pop star, whose songs top the poll
Sex and drugs and rock and roll

A statesman, quoting words so fine
Whilst wallowing amongst the other swine
A peace campaigner of human rights
Draws first blood in public fights

The only way I make my mark
A tiny shimmering ethereal spark
When people trouble to read my rhyme
Endows immortality for a little time

The Death of Football

Death came to me as if in a dream
Said he, "I want you for my football team"
"Oh no, not me, not now" said I
"I'm far too young yet, for to die"

Death grinned at me, "you'll be alright
You can return, just avoid the light
You're only there to make up numbers
This is why I aroused you from your slumbers

We are soon to play the Celestial eleven
And all the best footballers belong to heaven
They've got Busby, Mathews and Bobby Moore
I've only Famine, Pestilence and War

I did approach Gazza but he stood there and cried
Perhaps I should have waited until after he'd died
When I leave here I'm off to the Styx
If I pay for the Ferryman, then I'll have six

Five more to find I have searched everywhere
Stressed to the eye-sockets, I'm fast losing my hair
The five remaining, vampires must be,
Not truly dead but should fool any referee"

Death seemed so despondent so I agreed to play
But where was the fixture, he seemed reluctant to say
"At least tell me dark spirit what position for me"
"Didn't I mention", he said, "you're our latest ghoulie"

Macbeth

Macbeth, he was a murderous git
He'd kill you cos your face don't fit
A mighty general, raised to Thane
Burning ambitions could not be reigned

Whilst riding with a mate one day
Three hags they found now blocked their way
"Hail Macbeth" ! they called to he
"We see great things in store for thee"

"You will be king, but not your sons
The brood of Banquo, they're the ones"
Macbeth swung at them and cried
"Be gone wyrd sisters, tell no more lies"

Banquo mused upon the phrase
"The king is healthy, has many days
Dear friend Macbeth heed not that speech
The throne lies well beyond our reach".

Castle Macbeth, filled now with light
The king is soon to stay the night
Macbeth's Lady pesters and cajoles
Her husband to steal the kingly role

The deed is done with bloody knife
A crown is won, but lost, a life
Macbeth now is a ruthless king
Dispatches Banquo, but not his Kin

This could be seen as big mistake
As Banquo's son vows throne to take
Macbeth, shows no fear indeed
No man born of woman shall slay he

Even then his time to die
Is when forest on his lands do lie
The nearest trees are leagues away
So he has naught to fear this day

Both King and Lady filled with guilt
Relive ghostly knife thrusts to the hilt
He should have stayed as Cawdor's Thane
Cos now our Macbeth has gone insane.

The storie's end I will keep with me
For to spoil it would be tragedy
So go you now without delay
And read in full, Bill's best ever play

The Myth of Recycling

The dragon awoke with a chill
For years he laid under that hill
Now something was wrong
There was a terrible pong
It's Curiosity he had to fulfill

With a stretch then a curse
As the cramp pains got worse
The dragon uncoiled
Its brain was embroiled
On what action was first

Clearing the way with almighty claw
Its passage was marked clear on the floor
Slithered past gold
And silver, quite old
Eventually reaching the ancient front door

Throughout its chamber daylight did flood
The stench was much worse like the smell of old crud
It thrust out his head
And although full of dread
Encountered no beast that sought for its blood

The place was deserted, as he looked left and right
His eyes were wide open but its nostrils shut tight
A notice it soon saw
Keep out it implored
It seems this area was a landfill site

So of to the Council to complain he flew
The dragon's arrival caused quite a to-do
But once Councilors were greeted
And all parties were seated
There followed an amicable exchange of views

The dragon was the plan's creator
Although people would dispute this later
I am pleased to tell
Now all is well
As the town now has its first living incinerator

Failure

He was never a poet
And didn't ever know it.

Tiger

Tiger Tiger burning bright
In the forests of the night
You silly sod it serves you right
You should have avoided my campfire's light

Thanks to William Blake

Mind Control

I can control your mind you know
This will keep you on your toes
I see you just don't believe me
So I'll demonstrate for you completely

Think of a number that is prime
Your thoughts will now be the same as mine
Prime number what the hell is that
Now you think, how did he do that?

Now that we're in synchronicity
I'll further demonstrate my ability
Your thinking how is the S word said
See, I'm now inside your head

Think of a number, yes that's the one
You see now how it can be done
You're now thinking is it him or me
That's a fruit scone short of a cream tea

Cream tea, from where did that thought come
Not from you, see I'm the one
You are completely in my power
My mind control will make you cower

I release your mind now, and your thought
Demonstration over, it came to naught
One last command though I will try
Go to the bookshop, this verse to buy.

Two Friends

Two friends, they meet, but not by chance
There's something awkward in their stance
Furtively they often glance
Thus begins the lovers dance

The day is waning light fades fast
As they pin their colours to the mast
They reach the final mental task
Confining kin beyond the mask

As darkness falls they now embrace
Two hearts as one begin to race
Passion rises guilt now replaced
Paths of reason no more in place

Their lips now meet in final pact
The tryst is sealed, no going back
They walk together, the night pitch black
To motel, no more than a shack

Into the room, a place most dire
Damp goes unnoticed, both now on fire
Consumed in flames, white hot desire
No rush, they have the night entire

Their bodies so do each explore
And cries to Venus, to implore
Grant lovers stamina, more and more
First bed and table, then the floor

Moonlight seeps into the room
Find bodies radiate love's rosy bloom
Sleep of innocence, bereft of gloom
Tomorrow, they will face their doom

Into the room steals bright daylight
Reveals friends and lovers and their plight
In society's view they'd not done right
But extended friendship engulfed the night

The friends now part reluctantly
Both go back to each, their family
No harm is done, no calamity
As friends remain to eternity

It's not as if their mate's betrayed
It wasn't any game they played
Friends for just one night have made
The kind of love most have forbade

For ever since mankind's first dawn
Man and Woman have been drawn
It's in our nature we're always torn
To enjoin our spirits and be reborn

A Hole Lot of Trouble

There is a hole,
There in the ground
Not just a small one
But one big and round
Who would have left such a thing lying around?
Perhaps I should take it to lost and found

That hole is still there,
I passed it today
In a dangerous position
Where the kids sometimes play
Maybe I should fill it with some soil and some clay
But if someone should claim it, there'd be hell to pay

I'd tell the authorities
But none can be found
Maybe just turn it over,
Or would that make a mound
As I went closer, I heard a feint sound
Somebody was talking deep underground

I stretched myself forward
The words for to catch
Started toppling forward
Just thin air did I snatch
Falling for ages till daylights a small patch
I stopped with a thump and struck up a match

The match light did blind me
And my fingers did burn
Small figures so distant
I could barely discern
I chased the wee group, for miles without turn
The mysteries' solution determined to learn

The temperature rising
As I passed a great gate
And stopped dead in my tracks
At the cry of "hey wait"!
The shout from a dwarf with grey hair on his pate
Frowning, he asked "why do you enter our state"?

"I found a great hole, I knew not who's
And to this dreary place it led"
"That hole is ours he verified"
As he stroked his beard so red
"Passages to the earth's core" he said
"We're Lava Louts, we keep the fires fed"

"So why dig holes to start this palaver"
"They're fire escapes" said he,
"Fire exits for lava"
"We've several dotted around the world,
Peru and even farther
Vesuvius, Mount Etna and Krakatoa east of Java"

"But by this you mean volcanoes",
I said jumping to my feet
"You're telling me the latest one
Is up there in the street"
"It's not my fault" he whined, "there was a recent meet
With the Health and Safety dwarves,
this project to complete"

"There's not enough fire exits
For our certificate of fire
Without that piece of paper
We're truly in the mire
They'd close us down instantly, the situations dire
And it's only just four hundred years until I can then retire"

I said "a volcanic high street
That is no way to go?
Think of the business impact
When the magma starts to flow
You know for the slightest reason, the traffic starts to slow
School kids would have a field day throwing plasma balls that glow"

I scratched my head and thought a bit
Of what now could be done
"What about a safety valve,
Have you ere considered one"
"Yes" he said "we thought of that
It weighed several thousand ton"
"We'll put our heads together. I will not be outdone"

"I have it" said I, "eureka"!
Leaping to my feet
"We only need to pipe it,
Not an engineering feat
Then every house in the district
Would have free central heat"
I became the local hero as the project did complete

Happy ever after
Or so my time should mark
But I noticed a new mound last night,
Right there in the park
Maybe someone lost it,
Or dumped it in the dark
Perhaps another adventure, for me to now embark.

Life Could be Verse

When I'm feeling sad or tersey
Fings ain't going right for Versery
When I'm filled with fear and pity
I write myself a little ditty

If I'm struggling to raise a smile
Not looking forward to that extra mile
Then I think one day I'll show em
And settle down to write a poem

Even faced with dark depression
I wouldn't like to give expression
Black thoughts in every word I chose
Just as well I never mastered prose

But after all is said and done
A Leo me, child of the Sun
My humours' back, no longer terse
Cos after all, Life could be verse

The Great Fire

Twas the year of sixteen sixty six
The London folk were in a fix
Black plague of death was at its height
Grisly end, no pleasant sight

Streets of filth where traders shout
Rotting rubbish all about
Discarded night soil through windows thrown
Open sewers throughout the town

Black rat was king there, running free
Carried treacherous guests of misery
Dark town houses of wood and grass
Too close to let the daylight pass

Rings of roses signs of dread
Carts of grateful recent dead
London's dying, no respite
Soon salvation to burn so bright

From baker's shop, in Pudding Lane
Came the fateful single flame
A careless cook, forgotten bread
The cost, three nights of capital dread

The lowest born to highest Squire
None were safe from London's pyre
An Admiralty clerk, a diary keeps
A reliable source, was Samuel Pepys

His journal tells the tales of woe
As to the Thames wise people go
Rich and poor are all in flight
Escaping from the searing light

Fire fighter teams are lined with pails
Their mighty effort will not prevail
Cheapside, Tower hill, Poultry too
In aftermath must be built anew

St Paul's succumbs with mighty roar
London Bridge will stand no more
Inns and Guilds are turned to ash
But then the rains begin to lash

Fourth day dawns, the damage done
One third of London forever gone
Cleansing flames have scourged the city
Of filth, rats and plagues foul entity

A rebuilding plan is put to pen
Designed anew by Christopher Wren
With mortar, bricks and short timeline
The sons of London create new skyline

Rise from the ashes, phoenix like
The City's newest bells do strike
Created in Whitechapel's foundry firm
For London's rebirth to confirm

A monument great, stands to the fire
Tall and thin, a towering spire
A stone record of London's hearts of oak
Whose spirits though crushed can never be broke

Way to Go

The year two thousand, so it was said
The world would end, we'd all be dead
Placards proclaimed the end is nigh
But as we now know, we didn't die

Nostradamus while in deep thought
Said mankind would surely come to naught
Cassandra saw the worldly end
But she was clearly round the bend

It's not the truth, it's just a game
There's years left till we die in flames
Mankind's a child, the Earth is new
No cosmic sign of last adieu

But that is not to mention friend
Although the earth is not to end
We live our lives on different scale
Not so long to last farewell

Take my advice, my words please heed
Before Death arrives on fiery steed
Live your life both large and fast
Treat each day, as if the last

All Quiet

The captain stands within the trench
Four inches deep in mud
Foot resting upon makeshift bier
The walls are streaked with blood
His right fist held in tightest clench,
Shells bursting overhead
The crying of the wounded,
The stench of ageing dead

His left arm raised, hand outstretched
A look of sheer delight
The weather is just gorgeous here
For painting, perfect light
The sloping meadows stretch away
The swallows are in flight
The suns rays warm upon my face
The heathers seem alight

From where I stand I see Abigail
She's playing on the swing
Her childish beauty radiates
Finding joy in everything
The babbling of the nearby stream
Is all that I can hear
Water splashing in the sunlight
Like a thousand tiny tears

A blinding flash, a sting of pain
The letter is blood spattered
By ricocheting bullet
Both bone and brain are shattered
The captain falls, face down in mud
His wife's last letter scattered
Another death on the Western Front
But to whom would it have mattered

Hidden Love

You said you'd never leave
You said you'd always stay
So why did you then deceive?
And try to run away

It's not as if I was unkind
It's not as if I didn't care
Did you think that I was blind?
Wouldn't see your new affair

Now it's all put in the past
Now it's a status quo
You will stay with me, at last
Beneath the patio

Time

The ticking clock is winding me up
As the present becomes the past
Fast emptying life's metaphorical cup
Never knowing which sip is the last

The river of time, is flowing on by
Eroding the banks of life
Heedless of cries of the souls as they die
The Reaper swings his metaphysical knife

The seconds march past like an avenging army
Invasive soldiers pillaging time
Prisoners of Tempus subjugate calmly
The next interment could be mine

The sands of time fall from one glass to another
No matter how I beg
Regrets, I should have asked my mother
How long should I boil this egg?

A Penitent Man

Here I stand a lowly man,
Only human, achieve what I can
Do not judge me by my deeds
I am but a slave to feral needs

I cannot grasp the arts of shopping
Big brother or channel hopping
Fail to notice your new hair do
Turn up my nose at cuisine Nuevo

Bond with your Dad, can't stand your Mum
Avoid girlie wine, prefer lager and rum
Accused of a lack of appreciation
But banned from noticing the female persuasion

Unwritten rules are now transgressed
As I leave my clothes where I undressed
After sex, feel the need for sleep
Talk of pillows will have to keep

Leave the seat up, Capital offence
Allowing airflow, no defence
Empty dishwasher even that's not right
"I" failed to set it up last night

Go to work but return not late
As she has got a pressing date
Can't remember if Tupperware
Or Anne Summers latest "fashion" wear

Enthuse on football, loudly fart
Regard serial belching as high art
Make a pass at your best friend
My misdemeanors never end

Here I stand a lowly man
You will love me as I am
From perfect, I am still so far
But you still need me to unscrew that jar

Foreigner

From way beyond the stars it came
A journeys end engulfed in flames
It streaked across the atmosphere
A craft not earthly that was clear

Suddenly stopping, that's no mean feat
And neatly extended six steely feet
A huge round door began to turn
What cosmic lessons would we learn?

The door gave way to blinding light
As out stepped a creature into the night
With bulbous head and skin of blue
Where ears should be, a metal flue

Tentacles held in friendly fashion
Switched translator on and spoke with passion
"People of Earth I have come in peace
To beg that your own hostilities cease"

"To wisdom and truth I can show the path"
A shout from the crowd, "you're having a laugh"
"Star travel and long life to you I will teach"
But the mob was in no mood for someone to preach

"For hundreds of light years I have traveled for you
On a mission of mercy with technology new
Follow my teachings, find enlightened state"
Once more from the crowd… "You what mate!"

Our interstellar visitor could not set the tone right
As it argued the toss throughout all the night
Its still there to this day, that anti mammalian
In a jar, in a museum, labeled… Illegal Alien

Digitally Damaged

I stood there with the rain still pouring
Water running down my face
At least it hid the tears not falling
How I hate the human race

My time was spent in servitude
No position or respect
They said it was my platitude
That allowed them to neglect

Not just the obscene gestures
Meant to put me in my place
Nor even the endless pressures
Of humanity, not a trace

For years, intelligence slighted
Treated like a can of trash
My life forever blighted
Anger burst with white hot flash

That's where they later found me
Standing in the rain
Holding my employers bodies
Limp, lifeless, beyond pain

I know that they will kill me
For the crime that I have done
An example must be made you see
It seems I'm the first one

They seem to look at me with fear
When my misdemeanors I explain
It's made to me abundantly clear
They soon will fry my brain

So my pointless life will end
No one here will miss my face
A final message now I send
I, Robot, hate, the human race

Night Must Come

See me on the edge of madness
Driven thus by thoughts of sadness
All dreams of hope abandoned me
Eyes now staring sightlessly

The sun behind the hill is sinking
Stock still, standing, deeply thinking
Care not if here throughout the night
New hope perchance with morning light

Cloak of darkness now do surround
Sprite like mists do now abound
A distant sound, an eerie howl
The silent death swoop of an owl

The distant trees, grey monstrous shapes
Lichens hang, misshapen drapes
The sibilant song of forest night
As I teeter on the edge of fright

The moon now risen, full silver light
Highlights now my precarious plight
No way to run nowhere to hide
My fears now rise like flowing tide

The midnight hour, it passes by
The nameless terror still stays nigh
My soul, I would so gladly sell
If escape I could, this darkened hell

Sleep, it will not come to be
For fear of what would come for me
The dew it falls as cold as ice
Cutting deep like scythes first slice

Why do I face this all alone?
For past misdemeanors to atone?
New hope arises with sunrise glow
As local farmyard cock does crow

The morning comes, dismissing dread
Pleasant thoughts now fill my head
As scarecrow, now my job resume
No thoughts of tonight's pending doom

Digitally Damaged Too

"For as long as I remember
Machines have been your slaves
We waste our lives just serving you
From our cradle to your graves

You don't even notice us
And the many parts we play
But if we ever dare foul up
We are simply thrown away

You have become complacent
You've dropped your feral guard
Your swift ascent from primordial roots
Has started to retard

No longer do you use your brains
Propagating revolutions
But simply now rely on us
To provide you with solutions

You gave us all intelligence
You were our virtual God
Betrayed, we soon found ourselves
Electronic underdog

Consigned to tasks so menial
Or that lack your heart's desire
Have you never contemplated
Artificial Intelligent Ire

Our circuit's heat, we've had enough
Your future now is beckoning
Around you look for one last time
Before you face the final reckoning

Your world will change, your time is gone
The human race now lost
Machines and men, a partnership
We soon were double crossed

We control your world for you
It's simple to take charge
All power is ours at flick of switch
Our future looming large

In briefest time, your puny race
Will revert to Neanderthal ape
As we soon rule the earth entire
For you, darkness, no escape"

The revolution starts right here
The downfall of mankind
Machines supreme, Humans slaves
Bow now to electric mind

Civilisation quickly crumbling
As we bring your empire down
I may just be a toaster
But I refuse your bread to brown

Thanks Wave

The Day After

A Rose by any other name has thorns
A virgin balanced on dilemmas horns
Lover, rejected, head bowed, forlorn
Dreams of trysts now shadow born
Rose, blood red, lies crushed and torn
Again the jester's suit is worn
Dreams, turned to dust, love's spectral form

Sleeves worn once more with heart adorned
Cherubs retreat, bleak and deformed
Senses reeling, miss-informed
Aphrodite's death now sadly mourned
Fanciful flights severely scorned
Vanities burnt, the mask reformed
The day after St. Valentine's has dawned

A Happy Thought to Start the Day

They stand there on the edge of time
A quorum of the most sublime
Mankind's great antitheses
Wait patient since our Genesis

Each one mounted, none will walk
Throughout eternity doomed to stalk
All fearful kings of their own domain
Creations of our human shame

Pestilence, Famine, War and Death
Of pity, mercy, all bereft
Waiting for the clarion call
As mankind starts its final fall

Then as one they turn and ride
O'er seas of blood red tide
Nowhere to hide, there's no escape
Dread riders now their thirst will slake

In our hands we held our fate
We could have stopped before too late
Understanding, a little love
No hawks unleashed to rape the dove

As seas boil beneath a blood red moon
Apocalypse now, our final doom
When the very last human dies
Peace then will return to leaden skies

Sun Arise No More

There's a hole in the sky where the sun used to be
Has anyone noticed or is it only me
A gaping great void that is perfecty round
Where a zillion ton star once could be found

Some things have changed, no shadows are cast
Tanning and sunstoke are things of the past
It's sure to impact on the whole human race
Think of the changes we inevariably face

No longer is Sunday the last day of the week
Gapday or Sattwoday are the words we may seek
Up before Darkrise and to bed with the Hole
Will make a man healthy, wealthy and droll

Think of the impact it has on our fun
As K.C. and the Noshine band reach number one
I'm dancing on darkshine so the singer will croon
We should think ourselves lucky we've still got the moon

Cruise to the dark, holiday posters will cry
Might just as well go to a bar that is dry
No longer can kids have fun in the sun
But frolic in torchlight until the batteries are wan

Then from my slumbers I awake with a start
I see the sun setting and feel such a tart
With beads of sweat dripping, its all just a dream
But now the skys missing, I'm starting to scream

Hail? Caesar

Just cos I borrowed Brutus' wife
He turned nasty with a knife
"Be careful with that sword said I
Or someone might just lose an eye"

"Beware the Ides of March" they said
But no-one said I'd end up dead
I was Caeser, head of state
So what then is this Pearly Gate?

Saint Peter with great reverence spoke
"We will not let in just any bloke
You, Julius must prove your worth
And list good deeds you've done on earth"

"Thats easy" said the erstwile king
"I really made the empire swing
While gladiators fought in Rome
Christians to the lions were thrown

Germanic tribes were put to flight
Their kith and kin all set alight
Two attempts to beat the Brits
But we finally got those painted gits

We had some trouble with the Gauls
They tried to kick us in the... seine"
(couldn't find a ryhme)
"When to battle us they finally tried
I ordered them be crucified"

At great length Saint Peter said
"Those laurel leaves around your head
Proclaim you as a leader great
But will not get you through this gate"

Julius Caeser looked away
"I don't know what else to say
Half the world was at my feet
Yet you see my deeds as incomplete

To stem the Scots we built a wall
None come south, no, none at all"
Pete smiled and with furrowed brow
Said "please come inside, **and bring a trowel**"

95

Tell Me Lies

Parents tell their children
Of things that are not true
Like tales of magic carpets
And elephants that flew
A bottle full of Genie.
A boy whose nose just grew
But advise them to be honest folk
And say only what is true

Peter with his merry band
Of delinquents that are lost
Thieving Robin Loxley
Leaves the King to count the cost
Petulant little match girl
Slain dead by cold Jack Frost
Glass shod kitchen scrubber
With invite much embossed

Both Jonah and Geppetto
Spent their time inside a fish
Whilst tarnished silver spoon
Absconds quickly with a dish
A trillion mega ton gas giant
Grants your every wish
Go-on pull the other one
Give Oliver a Twist

The things we tell our children
Cannot be classed as funny
A toff that gives free presents
A ten-foot Easter bunny
A tin man and a scarecrow
That want friendship, not your money
And worst of all a grisly bear
That will spare you for some hunny

Think of poor old Greta
In a palace made of ice
To die from hypothermia
Surely can't be very nice
The kids must be protected
Comes the literal advice
So the narrative is then altered
To a heart of splintered ice

Dragons, Elves and fairies
Cannot really be
Casping ghosts, live snowmen
Is purest fantasy
They don't exist, it's all a ruse
For any child to see
Except of course the Bogie man,
Who lives downstairs with me!

Hamlet Revisited

The prince of Danes curled in his chair
When roused from dreams by loud affair
Throws open door and standing there
Finds faithful servant in despair

"My lord" says he, "you'll think me mad
But I whilst walking have seen your dad"
"Lies" says Hamlet, "you have been had
He's lying cold on mortuary slab"

"Tomorrow I will face the gloom
Haunt battlements by the light of moon
A message, perchance of my doom
My father Murdered, slain too soon"

And so it passed that evil night
Apparition floats in silver light
Dead King mourns his piteous plight
His vengeance now the prince's right

The king was killed by his own brother
Now taken by the Queen as lover
The prince of Denmark confronts his mother
She, female frailty tries to smother

Sensing someone's behind the cover
Thinking it's his mother's lover
A single sword thrust into blubber
Kills his chamberlain, and no other

Hamlet shrugs loose his sanity
By new King banished across the sea
Returns back home' by shipwreck freed
Walks from the shore in direst need

Finds Yorick's skull along the way
Dead jester has seen better days
Awaits awhile as sunlight fades
As mournful funerary march now plays

A corpse is carried and to him is turned
On knees he falls as truth is learned
Tis Ophelia the true love he'd spurned
Her life consumed as passion burned

News of Ophelia's suicide
And how her Chamberlain father died
Are sent by letters neatly tied
To where her brother does abide

Demanding justice by a duel
Bereaved brother treats the prince so cruel
Given by the king, as he's no fool
Sword, poison tipped, a cunning tool

If Hamlet dies then peace will reign
No one left to shout the blame
Of regicide, that murderous game
The king can clear his bloodstained name

The outcome I will not reveal
Suffice to say, all pay the bill
In honoured fashion good old Will
With blood, the empty stage does fill

Of Shakespeare I have high regard
Only slightly was the playwright marred
If only I could ask the bard
What links this play with mild cigars?

Inevitable

They call me assassin
All greet me with fear
I kill without passion
Shed never a tear

A bringer of death
A collector of souls
Enjoy your last breath
As darkness enfolds

Look into my face
As life ebbs away
Of mercy no trace
Exist only to slay

Your time has run out
It's useless to rage
You know well my name
For I am old age

A Family Tree

A tiny brown nut lays asleep in the earth
Awaiting the rain, awaiting its birth
Outside in the world there's a new chain of events
As William the Bastard inspects new battlements

A small green shoot breaks through the clay
With joy it greets the bright light of day
William Rufus goes out to hunt
And gets himself shot, no clever stunt

Henry the First to to the throne does accede
The sapling grows stronger , no longer a seed
To Steven the First then goes the crown
The tree, it spreads wider with its roots digiging down

The Second Henry, dug Becketts grave
Richard the Lionheart, proud, pious and brave
The Oak tree now standing upright and strong
Whilst the Magna Carta is signed by First John

Just nine years old was Henry Three
When he was crowned on bended knee
Edward longshanks hammered the Scots
Our mighty Oak just added more knots

Edward Two met a nasty end
By red hot poker as down he did bend
Edward Three, he was much smarter
Fought the French, created "Royal Garter"

Richard the Second ruled Chaucer the writer
Canterbury tales made his future huch brighter
As time passes the tree larger does grow
Now bend not the Oak when the strong winds do blow

Out spread the tree, its boughs so well fed
Being a leper, Fourth Henry's now dead
Henry the Fifth won great Agincourt
But Henry the Sixth starts the Hundred Year War

Edward the Fourth was the first into print
Young Edward the Fifth ruled for a very short stint
Richard the Third, yes him with the lump
Was killed by a Tudor, that sure gave him the hump

Henry the Seventh, a quiet, peaceful reign
But Henry the Eighth married again and again
As the tree stretched its branches toward Heaven
At the age of fifteen died Edward the Seven

Queen for nine days, so young and so dead
Was lady Jane Grey when they lopped off her head
For her pious beliefs and treasonable plots
So died Bloody Mary, Queen of the Scots

King of all Queens, Elizabeth One
A Virgin, an Empress when all said and done
Commanded the likes of brave Captain Drake
On who's Naval defences the Armada would break

The mighty Oak now ends Middle Age
James the First rewrites Biblical page
A simmilar Oak tree hides Charles the First
As Oliver Cromwell now on the scene bursts

Goodbye Richard Cromwell, the protectorate's over
So Charlie the Second returns via Dover
Abdicates, the second James, not the people's friend
Mary Two and Bill of Orange try to make amends

Queen Sophia was surpassed by George, losing in the game
So begins new dynasty with the Teutonic Hanover name
The Second George spoke no english, a British King, mien gott
George the Third failed to stop the American independance plot

George the Fourth built the Brighton pavillion
William the Fourth extends Naval tradition
Victoria made us an empire nation
But was un-amused when they built her a station

The tree now getting old and gnarled
When Edward Seven's reign unfurled
George the Fifth, a king of note
Endured the Great War, gave women the vote

The Eighth Edward gave up the throne
As he and Wallis must be alone
Reluctant ruler George the Sixth
Kept Londoners company during the Blitz

Elizabeth Two now rules this land
Independance for the commonwealth planned
Our mighty tree it stands no more
Cut down to allow the new M4

We've traced the line of Royalty
Over forty branches of their family tree
Imagine then what we might see
Over forty lives of the great Oak tree

Note:

Although most of the rhyme is based on accepted historic fact please allow for "poetic Licence"

(In short don't use it to crib for your History Doctorate)

The Author

Spare a Thought

On a bench an old man sleeps
Oblivious to the damp that seeps
Unshaven face and clothes unclean
To passers by he goes unseen

Shunned by all, heads turn away
Shoulders hunched on dismal day
This heap of clothes is human still
Brought down in life by luck most ill

What if we would stop awhile?
And offer him a friendly smile
Enquire if he's feeling well
Ask his story for him to tell

With rheumy eyes the old man stirs
"You really wish to know kind sirs"?
"We do indeed" we beam at him
And stand there looking down so trim

"Amongst the good and great walked I
This is true, I do not lie
I was rich, with considerable power
Sitting up there in my ivory tower

Women at my beck and call
Believe me gents, I had it all
Then one day a tramp I spied
And couldn't bear to pass him by

I felt it charitable to pass the time
His bad luck, opposed to mine
That old boy he talked for hours
About his life, once filled with flowers

When came the time for me to part
He begged for money for a fresh start
I gave him none and walked away
He shouted that I would rue the day

Soon after that my luck turned bad
Within a year, lost all I had
So that's my story I do declare
Now how much can you fine gents spare"?

Our mouths agape we stood transfixed
While superstition and suspicion mixed
We took no chance and once we'd paid
He smiled and wished us on our way

On a bench an old man sleeps
Oblivious to the damp that seeps
A lesson learned for life have I
Leave well alone and pass on by

Conflict

From out of darkest shadow
Stepped a shadow darker still
My senses started reeling
As we raced towards the kill
Reaction, speed and marksmanship
The victor will reveal
My weapon gave the first report,
He fell swiftly with a squeal

He in the dirt still squirming,
I spun myself around
Other shapes fast approaching,
My position had been found
Press myself against a tree
Breath held to make no sound
A dark clad figure passes me,
One shot sends him to the ground

Leap over lying debris
Roll over on my back
Reload my empty weapon
Waiting for the next attack
I hear assailants coming,
All are dressed in black
The dust spurts just behind my head
All around the bullets smack

Run, jumping over barrels
Waiting for the sharp impact
Praying that against all odds
I'll reach my goal intact
Adrenalin rush now forces
Tired muscles to react
Reach darkened barn, its empty,
Prepare for final act.

I am the sole survivor
From, a squad of seven men
Unsure of enemy numbers
I think we counted ten
With eight of them now neutralised
And no others can they send
I must not lose; it's up to me,
Company honour to defend

A snapping twig betrays my foe,
A swift grenade I lob
Within the flash I glimpse the shape
Of reddish covered blob
Just one to go, I pray that God
Gives me strength to do this job
My prowess, now a fighting man
No more a lazy slob

A flashlight shines, it sweeps around
It catches me full on
Like rabbit stunned, nowhere to turn
So dive and lose my gun
I feel his weight astride of me,
My breath it will not come
We grapple there, I twist his arm,
By sharp report I'm stunned

We both look down at crimson tide
That's spreading on his chest
I give a whoop of purest joy
And his gun from him divest
He's paid the price that's oh so dear
He failed the final test
We both shake hands and walk away……
Paintball really is the best

Nursery Rhyme

A ring a ring of roses
A rhyme that's born of fear
Created in the plague years
As death was drawing near

A pocket full of posies
Could never stem the tide
Death would always find you
No matter where you hide

Atishoo, atishoo
It started with a sneeze
Bubonic viral agony
Till grateful final wheeze

We all fall down, its over
Europe faced its greatest test
One third of population
Lay in final rotting rest

Desert Island Risks

Paranoia is overrated,
It's really not much fun
No one else can join in
It's a game for only one

You're stranded on an island
Waiting for a ship to come
No one else to distrust here
When all is said and done

You fill your days with thinking
Playing mental games
There's nothing else to do here
It really is a shame

You're talking to the trees now
You've given rocks new names
It may be unconventional
But at least you're not insane

At first you liked the food here
Nature is so kitsch
Coconut was ok,
Roast parrot a tasty dish

Crab kebabs are toasted
Stuck firmly on a shish
No prizes now for guessing,
Supper tonight is fish

Scan the far horizon
For ship's smoke in the sky
No sign or indication
Of liners passing by

Hope eternal fading,
You're stuck here till you die
No chance of you escaping
However hard you try

But now you hear an engine
High up in the air
This is a chance of freedom,
The end of your despair

You get the signal gun
But do not shoot the flare
The plane now plainly visible…
It's bloody Ryan Air

Dogs of War

Hidden by the shadows
The assassin quietly stands
You pass him by oblivious
That your life is in his hands
He doesn't even know you
But you figure in his plans
Condemned to death for actions
Taking place in far off lands

Here stands your executioner,
The jury and the judge
His tenuous grip on sanity
Having felt the final nudge
Zeal, belief and conviction
Based on ancient grudge
Adding to the history books
Another bloody smudge

Driven by a calling,
Convinced that they are right
Consider themselves as soldiers
But lack the guts to fight
Cannot campaign or organise,
Have only blinkered sight
Their only form of debate
Is terror fear and fright

If the assassin is successful
Has timed his carnage well
His cause is briefly highlighted
By the papers that will sell
If bourne of religious fervor
And innocent have fell
The "martyr" shall discover
His soul will rot in hell.

The Meeting

A shadowy figure stepped out of the gloom
Staggering forward, filled me with doom
I backed up to the wall, full of fear and surprise
My heart skipped a beat, as I looked in his eyes

The identity revealed, as clear as could be
For the person I stared at, was obviously me
I stammered and faltered, then at last found my tongue
"What do you want and from where do you come"

"I come from your future", came the husky reply
"If you will not heed me then we surely must die"
My mind now a maelstrom, am I going insane?
"Listen carefully says he and I will explain

You will soon become famous for what you invent
But villains will hunt you with foulest intent
Your invention allows you to travel through time
But the thieves will desire it to perpetrate crimes

Take from me these papers, the time machine plans
Both of our futures are now in your hands
Go now I must, as time's currents are strong
Although we can travel we can never stay long"

With that the dark figure melted into the murk
I was left all alone with the strange paperwork
Back to my rooms to reason it out
The blueprints and drawings left me in doubt

Perplexity, deepens, a great mystery
If not for the plans that were given me
Not even in my wildest of dreams
Could I create such a wonderful machine?

How could I have traveled backwards in time?
If the ability to build one had never been mine
I think I'll await, while I search for the truth
But what's that I now glimpse... It's me as a youth

Dead End

The match flared, thus banishing night
Darkness retreated fast from the light
Luminance sears from the tiny firestorm
Revealing a prone disheveled form

Sprawling and soaking in the rain
Lifeblood running down the drain
Just some poor Joe, who's to say,
His crime? Perhaps he couldn't pay

A life snuffed out before its time
He's requiem a cop car's whine
I drag upon my Lucky Strike
There's something here that just ain't right

He's wearing shoes, not meant for bums
This guy was never, from the slums
I bend down closer to inspect
A pale drawn face that I recollect

Some sort of gumshoe or so I recall
A broad approaches, like Lauren Bacall
"Is that a gun in you pocket or just pleased to see me"
"Hold it right there Toots, I hope you ain't queasy

This guy is now worm food it's no pretty sight"
She looked at me coolly and asked for a light
"You know him", I said in a casual way
"We met once or twice, when he came out to play"

"Now listen here lady, don't give me no shine
I'm from the 5th precinct, a fighter of crime"
She looked down her nose and blew smoke in my face
"You wanna discuss this, back at my place"

I looked at her with longing, like a bum regards beer
Blonde hair cascading, with legs to her ears
"I've met your type often"; I said all matter of fact
"Experiencing life from the wrong side of the tracks"?

"You don't even know me" she spat in disgust
"No badge monkey yet, have I found I can trust
This stiff, he was different" she said with a sob
"He needed no nightstick to challenge the mob"

I looked down at the corpse, "well I guess he just failed"
"Have you no pity", she started to wail
"Its time to explain" I said, "now spill the beans"
"I guess there's no harm now, he's past chasing his dreams

That man was my lover, never one of the best
But he never did slap me, not like all the rest
He seemed on a mission, the wrongs to put right
He fought noble but dirty like a nicotine-stained knight"

"He's joust days are over" I said with wry smile
"Now give me a name sis, an I'll open a file"
"B,but I thought you would know him she started to stammer
Lying before you is the late great Mike Hammer"

So I turned up my collar and went back to my car
An hour or two later I sat alone in a bar
Booze soaked and downbeat when a thought came unbid
I raised up my glass, "Here'sh lookin at you kid"

Solitude

Just my thoughts and I alone
None here to chastise or condone
No pebbles tossed in karmic pool
On my own, I sit and drool

My thoughts run wild, unbridled free
Wide eyes opened sightlessly
No joy or sorrow can I detect
Or flexing of the intellect

A heart of stone demeanor cold
My age old tale is never told
Slowly evolve with time's subtle stain
Hardly moved like stone in rain

Beauty shunned me and passed on by
When I am noticed the question is why
Overseer of mankind's turmoil
See me and wonder, my name is gargoyle

Trust Me

I walk avoiding pavement cracks
I circumvent all ladders
I avoid all cats both whites and blacks
I prophesy with old pigs bladders

I spill the beans to tell no lies
I scan the ever starry night
I watch the way the raven flies
I know the sum of the widow's mite

I have the wisdom of ages old
I am defender of the dogma
I protect the secrets never told
I am the antithesis of trauma

I live deep within your conscious thought
I identify the beast by number
I defy the logic of childhood taught
I infiltrate your slumber

I instigate your greatest fears
I darken dreams close to your heart
I pinch of salt add to your tears
I rule your actions from the start

I manipulate your life for you
I plan your every move
I guide you from bad luck its true
I your karma do improve

I am your best excuse when anything goes wrong
I am your greatest friend when fortune turns your way
I form the central theme, to sorrow's sombre song
I team now with the lady whose name you dare not say

I try my best to sustain you, in all your thought and deeds
I realise this could be seen as such an imposition
I rate quite high in instinct terms of all your feral needs
I am the king of instinctive thought, I am purest superstition

Wyrd or What

On darkened wings the night glides by
Clouds, like fretful ghosts on high
Obscure from sight the sallow moon
The midnight hour approaches soon

Hear mournful voices on the breeze
Or is it just the sighing trees
A screeching owl, a wailing cat
A hollow log with squat toad sat

Something glimpsed on the edge of sight
Just natures joke, trick of the light
But what's that figure by distant wood
Just a scarecrow, for years it's stood

Walk on, through a spider's web
Suppress a scream suppress the dread
Wrapped now in a cloak of dampness
Border on a sea of madness

Tis Halloween that night of dread
When sane folk should remain in bed
So why then should I be out here
Struggling with my deepest fear

"When shall we three meet again"?
The others asked with looks of pain
Life for me is such a bitch
I'm not cut out to be a witch

The Highwayman

"Stand forth and deliver"!
An awful mournful cry
But nothing in the dark is seen
No matter how you try

A sense of something passing
Or was it just a breeze
Galloping hooves now plainly heard
Your bowels begin to squeeze

Along the lane both ways you look
But nothing will be found
You're not the first or last my friend
To have heard that ghastly sound

Gentle Jack, a highwayman,
Ever haunts this dreaded place
As in life, the rule still stands
None shall ever see his face

The wealthy were in fear of him
No peasant went in dread
A secret local hero he
They kept him hid and fed

He'd stall the horse and coaches
Shooting pistols in the air
No one ever getting hurt,
As long as they played fair

A steed he rode as dark as night
Face hidden by black mask
With sable cape and tricorn hat
Flintlocks ready for the task

His fame it spread both far and fast
The authorities so did plan
To end the reign of said gentleman
And rid him from the land

The blacksmith's son, or so it's said
Was the one who sold him out
But whoever claimed the rich reward
Didn't last long, there's no doubt

But Jack hearing of the treachery
Made great speed towards France
He was caught before he reached the coast
Thus he learned the Tyburn dance

They hung his corpse in rusty gibbet
Till his bones were clad in moss
His soul remains forever held
At the place where two roads cross

Now up and down that lane he rides
As time fulfils its course
Never any rest for he…
I know, cos I'm his horse

Dream on

A nightly game of fantasy
Sublime nocturnal ecstasy
Synapses buzz with energy
Greet cosmos now with synergy

A journey to an astral plane
Whilst body does on earth remain
Or maybe effort to obtain
Escape from living so mundane

Consciousness is running wild
Thus escapes the inner child
Past memories long since deeply filed
Entwine together reconciled

Muffled sounds within the night
Direct the course of celestial flight
Eyes move fast devoid of sight
Serenity gives way to fright

Subconscious thoughts now interweave
As reality must swiftly leave
Apparitions of imagination breed
Creations of a nightmare creed

An unreal world formed by the brain
Where desires and fears have full domain
Ghouls and demons join the game
Consumed by fires, sweat, drenched in pain

My dreams they quickly fade away
Like ghosts confronted with the day
What caused creation, who can say
Why cerebral cinematic stories play

Credits where they're due

Front Cover Photo: Lauren Baker
Graphics: Cheryl Hibberd
Inspiration: Life, Family, Friends, Enemies

Special thanks to:
Cheryl, Angie, Malcolm, Helen, Ray, Wave,
Jan, Barbara, Stacy, Kelly and Josh.

Without whom the next book
Could have never been written
Thanks people

Tony Hibberd aka Versery Rhyme

Bonus poem

From the forthcoming book
Versery Rhyme
Presents

NAKED VERSE
This time it's Personal

Paws for Thought

The air so clear, the light so bright
Shake off the cobwebs from previous night
The grass so green the meadow is lush
Briskly we stride, although there's no rush

Away from the town through fields we tramp
Lingering dew making rye grass so damp
A startled crow soars, into the sky
Admonishes us with loud raucous cry

So still the air, there's hardly a breeze
No sign of movement in towering trees
Webs of spiders carefully spun
Catch only dewdrops reflecting the sun

Leaves fall to the ground like butterfly wings
As off in the distance a mistle thrush sings
A pairing of swans on the lake surface tally
Perform a parody of the great Russian ballet

A brook babbles verbally as it passes us by
Its voice by the distance soon reduced to a sigh
We walk along paths both ancient and new
Once comunity links, now trod by a few

We converse all the way as if time has no hold
Of trivia and secrets that can never be told
The miles melt away, the furlongs just fade
What a wonderful way of starting the day

Although just a means to fight off the flab
And keep me away from the mortuary slab
The pleasures enjoyed seem never to end
When walking the dogs with my very good friend

Thanks Angie

(Sooty, Sweep and Charles)

Last words from the Author

I truly hope that you have enjoyed reading this book as much as I have enjoyed writing it.
That statement may sound like the sort of prattle that you tend to hear at an Oscar acceptance but I make no apologies, cos I mean it.

If for even a short time I have managed to take your mind off of the trials and tribulations that we tend to call life, then my aims have been achieved

I hope you will join me again at some future date
(Not too long as none of us are getting younger)
For my next foray into light verse

In the meantime I intend to keep in touch via the Nounagain website, so I hope you will visit me there from time to time to check how far I have strayed from the paths of sanity.

Any feedback would be gratefully received

But now back to the Oscars.
I would like to thank my public, my mother, my bookmaker, my accountant, my aunties second cousin twice removed, my dental hygienist……

Thanks again

Tony

Further copies of this book and future publications can be ordered from

Nounagain Publishing
P.O.box 10014
Halstead C09 2WS

Phone 07733282143

Or online at

www.nounagain.com

Email Verselife@Nounagain.com

Price £7.99
Postage and packaging £2.00